Dec 2017

Dear Fran

Some good thoughts for you,
not just for Christmas. But also for
Christmas.

Love

Ruth x

On Art and Mindfulness

notes from the Anderson Ranch

Enrique Martínez Celaya

AndersonRanch
arts center

On Art and Mindfulness

notes from the Anderson Ranch

Enrique Martínez Celaya

Whale & Star Press

Anderson Ranch Arts Center

For Ulrich and Harriet Meyer

Contents

The six illustrations in this volume
are reproduced from original ink drawings
by the author

Preface

Every summer between 2005 and 2013 I offered a workshop at the Anderson Ranch Arts Center in Snowmass, Colorado. These workshops included critique sessions, painting classes, and lectures on art and theory. The Ranch attracts artists from all over the world ranging from those who have just finished graduate school to many who have been working for decades. One of these artists was the painter, Irene F. Sullivan, who during each of those summers took notes on what I said during lectures, critiques, and conversations; it is on her notes that this book is based.

I have edited the original comments to eliminate repetition, but I have retained similar remarks when they touched on what I considered to be different aspects of an idea. The comments have been arranged into topics that might be relevant to artists and to those interested in art, and when a comment could be placed in more than one category, I chose the one I considered most appropriate. It would be best, however, not to think of these topics as definite boundaries but only as a few of the many possible navigation marks one can place on the material.

The book is primarily about mindfulness rather than about affirmation or findings. The work of an artist unfolds in the experience of wrestling with the moment, so reminders to be aware of and responsive to those qualities and attitudes that make an artist an artist is often useful and always urgent.

My gratitude goes to the Anderson Ranch Arts Center and to the people I met there; to my wife, Alexandra, and to my children who often came with me to Colorado; to Harley Baldwin and Richard Edwards who first brought me to Aspen; to María Teresa Bonilla, Tessa Blumenberg, and Mary Strebinger who helped with the compilation and editing of the manuscript; and to Irene F. Sullivan, who without her careful recordings of what I thought were passing remarks, this book would not exist.

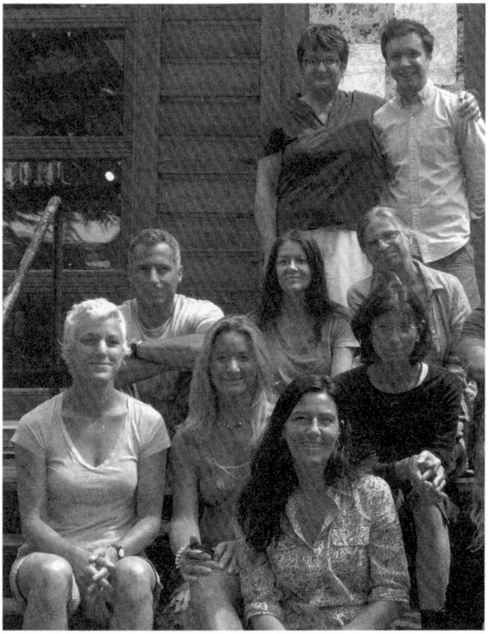

Anderson Ranch Arts Center, 2012

On Art and Mindfulness

Being an Artist

Being an artist is not a posture or a profession but a way of being in the world and in relation to yourself. An artist is revealed in his or her choices. Watch your actions as well as what you like and notice who is the person suggested by them. Understanding who you are as an artist should be thought of as a life-long process inseparable from your work.

There is often uncertainty in the choices an artist must make. In order to navigate this uncertainty and to use it to the benefit of your work, you should aim to have a clear mind and be aware of everything that conspires against that clarity.

Self-aware artists are confident but humble in relation to their work. Confidence encourages you to take risks while humility helps you to be skeptical of your own opinions, tastes, insights, stories, accomplishments, and virtue, including the virtue of your humility. And when humility and confidence come along with an appreciation for reality as it is, you will find it easier to be light in your attachments, bold in your thoughts and actions, and reverent in your attitude.

Growth does not have to be systematic. The way of the artist is a meandering path.

Sometimes we consider something to be new when, it is not. Learn as much as you can and try to keep in mind how little you know. Reverence for knowledge comes from appreciating what you know while recognizing how little you in fact know.

You must have your eyes open. The habit of looking at things with curiosity should carry through in everything you do. Marvel is all around you.

If you are not sophisticated you should not pretend to be. An artist should not be a pretender. It is better to have a lesser knowledge that is earned than a greater one that is borrowed. You can only bring work forth from your own level of experience. You will fool many people by impersonating a deeper spirit, a smarter mind, but the work knows—and shows you—where you are.

There is much attention placed on talent, but when trying to do something significant, character and devotion are the determining factors of success.

Urgency drives the artist; and urgency, tenacity, and unreasonableness go hand in hand. Cowardice often comes dressed as reasonableness.

All of us want to be there already, and so we make our plans and judgments based on that, but usually we are not there yet. We must persevere. Even though urgency drives the artist, patience is also important.

It is helpful to attend schools and workshops, but artists are ultimately self-taught, and it is the intensity and quality of this self-education that makes the difference.

Ask yourself, "What is it that I know?" Then be skeptical of the answer and ask the question again. To grow as an artist you must be able to rediscover your work each day by remaining in awe of the possibilities and of what is in front of you.

The first question an artist should think about is, "Why create art?" The answer to this question usually offers direction.

Every once in a while you should ask yourself, "Why not work another way?" In trying to find an answer, or even a general sense of an answer, you will gain insight into your work and you will challenge its foundations. "Why is my response to the work not qualitatively different?" is a good question to ask oneself, but not an easy one.

The moment we start thinking we know what kind of work we are doing, we are giving up the responsibility for the inquiry. This responsibility demands that each day we find again what the work is and what it means to us.

Art depends on fine distinctions. Develop your ability to make them, but you should not become an expert in your choices. Be willing to surprise yourself.

Some choices precede an action and some are made after the action has already taken place. Deciding what you leave in and what you take away is a choice, maybe the most difficult choice. Everything in a work of art is a choice.

How convinced are you of what you are doing? Be careful how you answer this. Conviction cuts both ways.

It is useful to ask, "What is the purpose of the work?" and also, "What is the purpose of one's work in the world?" The artist must not lose track of his purpose. What is the use of your work for you? Is it the same as the purpose of your work? To consider purpose, to understand what you want, engage with great works of art. Let them show you the way.

When we think we know art, what is it that we know?

An artist must always be a student of art. Each encounter with art should be an opportunity to learn how to be an artist.

Freedom, doing what we want, and responding to our whims are what we consider our birthright as artists, but we are always serving something or someone. Do not let that service be a mystery. Make it a choice.

Become familiar with your reactions to art but do not use them to construct a dogma.

We are all lying to ourselves to one degree or another. It is important to have a sense of our own lies.

Hearts tend to appreciate what they already harbor as dear so their approval does not mean much. For most people, the gut, the heart, and common sense, are poor guides of the unknown, the spectacular, and the surprising.

Work on polishing your intuition. Few people are born with perfect emotional pitch.

Reason and the gut must work together if anything meaningful is to be made. The best way to encourage this cooperation is to remain unbalanced in relation to yourself. Do not trust your own story. Your position will change over time and shift with your own discoveries, so we should not think of intuition as an unchanging ability but as something that is polished through experience.

There will be times in which you will have to be extreme. These moments are difficult if you look back, but are easier if you look forward.

Give up comforts and assurances to discover who you are without them.

Is there anything in your work that you are willing to risk your life for? To let yourself be shamed for? If not, then what is your work? To be an artist you need vulnerability, and being willing to be vulnerable in the face of challenges, the expectations of others, and your own accomplishments, requires courage.

The places in which you are fragile and vulnerable are good sources for your work.

When doubts bring you down, go back to the work not with the intention of doing something great but of doing something that marks your presence, that affirms you exist. Do not let yourself remain absent.

Artists work for years on what they think they should. Sometimes this is how they miss their real calling.

You do not have to be a scholar-artist. Many great artists were not. But if that is what you want to do, then be serious. Do not dabble.

Practice your judgment. Do not suppress it. Judge ideas not people. Take a position. If it is wrong, you will know soon enough. Do not be afraid to articulate your point of view. It is necessary so you can see how much improving it needs.

Look at your assumptions often. Chances are you will find your mistakes there.

Many artists are confident at the surface and insecure at the core, which makes them scared of going too far off course. Aim to be insecure at the surface and confident at the core. In this way you will question everything you do without fear you might get too far off course. You might, but you will be fine.

There is no comfortable foundation for an artist to stand on. Do not look for it, and if you find it, get off it.

Being critical with yourself is different than self-disparaging. The aim of being self-critical is not to destroy self-confidence, but to build it on the right foundation.

The more you protect what you have attained, what you are known for, what you think your work is about, the less likely you will create something extraordinary.

Your strength as an artist does not have to come from your best qualities or gifts. An artist can rise from a deficiency within himself or herself.

Put aside irony. Irony is hostile to reality. Irony camouflages confusion and cowardice. It postpones engagement. The comfort of irony is a false comfort.

Assume the world is likely to break you so instead of finding a place to hide, develop the strength to persevere.

Art has the possibility of redemption, but not every artwork or every practice is redemptive.

Line up your desires with your actions.

There are rewards in solitude but understand why you seek it. Isolation can be a way to hide in the safety of your own beliefs.

Art tends to be a solitary experience for the artist, but it becomes less so if you have some relationship with nature and if your work is connected to life.

Find beacons to guide you. You will need them. Treasure the good findings. Reject the bad ones. You do not have to explain your choices.

Take your time. Do not gel too quickly. Do not try to find your voice or your style. Instead, open your eyes and try to see what is in front of you.

Some artists try to be aware of and responsive to the values they consider to be the right ones and they construct their lives based on them. If you are one of these artists, let your life be its own reward, but do not expect art to respond to the thoughtful life you have set up for yourself. Art does not care about your sacrifices, which in some cases can be considerable. It does not offer consolation prizes for effort. It will ignore your kind gestures and the nice trees you planted in the backyard, and it seems to have no respect for how long you have been at it.

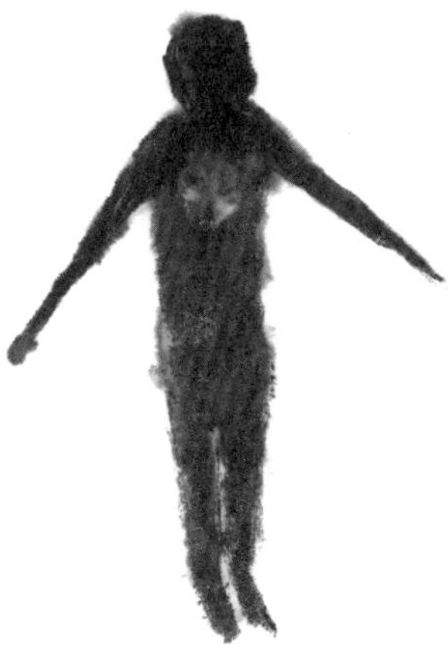

Art as Experience

Art is an experience—not a thing or an activity—which unfolds in the confrontation with the work of art, and in the case of a great work of art, the experience is somewhat like watching a locomotive go by: you see it coming and think you know what to expect. Maybe you tell yourself you have seen many locomotives before. Yet, when it goes by, you are nonetheless startled by its power.

A great work of art is both standing against itself and its own self-justification. Greatness in art is born from tension rather than from stability.

Art is as much about what is not there as about what is there. The greatness of a work of art depends more in what it holds back than in what it shows.

Art lets truth originate, but art and truth are evolving events, not fixed locations. Art is always in conflict with itself. Truth manifests in that conflict, but it is not stable—it is constantly undoing itself. The truth of art is held by a thin thread that dissolves if you hold it too tightly. Explaining the process of bringing a work about or its iconography and explaining the truth of the work are different things.

Art reconciles the conceptual and the sensible and makes connections between ideas and world that are difficult to make otherwise. It reconciles aspects of experience that are rarely considered together. Take Michelangelo's *Pieta*: Is it marble? Is it death? Is it loss? Is it compassion? The power of the sculpture rises from the co-existence of all these questions.

At the beginning of their creation, artworks are bound to the human. As they evolve, the human is shed so the artist can emerge. The more something is bound to the human, the less it is art, yet great art must always go through the human.

Most of us look at art the way art history taught us to look at it. Recover looking at art as an artist. Stop talking about art in bulk. There is El Greco and there is Manet. What does one gain from lumping them together? Art is always a specific instance.

An artist like Albert Pinkham Ryder makes paintings that ought not to work, but they do. Why they work is a mystery worth considering.

When standing in front of an artwork, do not ask who made it or which gallery does the artist work with. Simply ask yourself, "Is this work moving me? Is it revealing something?" Answering these questions is not always easy. Put aside the art historical interpretations for a moment, but stay conscious of how the work was made.

We have expanded the category we call art to include many things. It is probably true that anything can be art, but most things are not art.

Art is a testimony of having lived—maybe the most convincing testimony.

It is not taste that recognizes art but spirit.

What argument can you put forth to defend something being art to some degree? I don't think there is any. There is no good art or bad art. Art is or it is not.

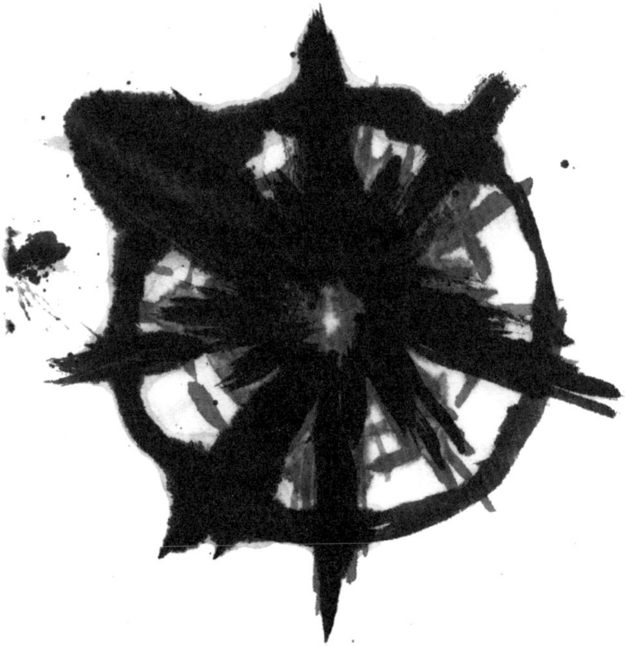

Words tend to distance us from experience, but words can, at times, get us closer to experience. This apparent contradiction suggests there must be different kinds of words or different groupings of them.

Language can be used to build other things. Art cannot be used this way. It is an end in itself.

Ambition and instability go hand in hand in a great work of art. The moment an artwork becomes stable, known, it becomes less ambitious and it ceases to be art.

There is no description, no adjective, no attack, no attribution of a certain quality, that will always be negative or always positive independently of the artwork to which it relates. To many, the idea of calling something dynamic, for instance, is a compliment, but some works are not meant to be dynamic. In art, everything is an instance. Every work proposes its own values.

Paintings are understood experientially, so if you shrink a painting, for example, everything changes: Edges, relationships, handling. What changes the most is your stance—where that work is coming from.

Good paintings are never what they seem. In good paintings, what we think we recognize soon becomes mysterious. In lesser paintings, what at first seems mysterious we recognize rather soon.

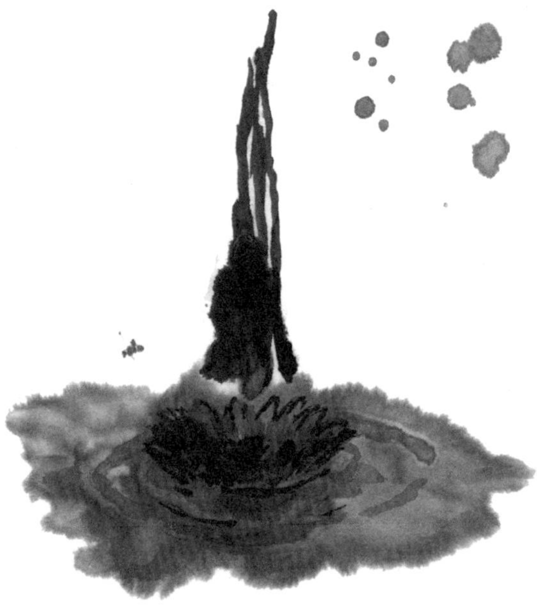

Consider painting as a noun instead of as a verb. Think of it as an object of the mind rather than a vessel for, or a record of, the things you do to it. Those who view painting as a verb tend to approach it in terms of actions—strokes, gestures, movement. Those who view painting as a noun tend to see the work as a mental state, which widens the scope of what a painting can be.

Two works could have similar choices, execution and subject matter, and still remain far apart.

Art can have many roles and can be of great use to you and to others, but those roles and those uses do not necessarily mean the art is good.

Take the following sequence: 1, 3, 6, 10, 15, 21. You may or may not know the next number in the sequence is 28, but the order is there whether or not you are able to recognize it.

Art is not a democratic enterprise and has little to do with fairness or with good intentions.

Notes on Ethics

What you say about your ethics is not as significant as what you do and how you do it. You should seek your own ethics as well as your own morals rather than borrow them from one canon or another. Ethics can be thought of as an algebra of resistance and acceptance, of what you are willing to fight and willing to embrace. The ethics of an artist are visible in his or her work.

Camus wrote that freedom, rather than being made up principally of privileges, is made up of duties. This is clearly true of the freedom of standing in front of an artwork.

He also wrote in *Resistance, Rebellion, and Death*, "If, after all, men cannot always make history have a meaning, they can always act so that their own lives have one."[1]

Put integrity ahead of convenience. Prioritizing integrity will serve you well, especially in those moments when you feel you have nothing else to rely on. In talking, never say anything specific about your ethics. What we care about is what you do and how you live. The choices you make reveal your ethics as well as your stamina in confronting doubt.

Wide acclaim is not needed for something to be true.

Regret and lost time are hard to deal with. Sometimes we feel things have not worked out as we had hoped. But there is always the opportunity of the present moment.

The qualities that distinguish great art from the rest are, directly or indirectly, related to ethics. At the heart of great art you find love and compassion. Great art is a result of internal tautness. The undercurrent of softness one feels in many works is related to insufficient love. A great work of art cannot come from hatred or cynicism.

Recognizing their work has no power, some artists spend their time introducing devices, flourishes, or pretensions to dissimulate and confuse their limitations. The same time and effort could be used trying to summon courage.

Freedom is elusive and frequently it is not where we think it ought to be. Much time is devoted to talking about freedom in art, but art is mostly about boundaries. About constraints.

To remain authentic you must fight against the cynics and the tired, and also against your own sense of accomplishment.

If you have an inclination towards philosophy and art theory, then you should engage them seriously, but do not take on theory as décor to validate your practice.

Every artist struggles with the balance between simplicity and complexity, as well as with the tension between similarity and difference. Your life and work will document how you navigate these dualities.

As an artist you have an opportunity to reconcile the conceptual and the sensible. That reconciliation might help you rediscover the radiance of your world.

The term "aesthetics" is frequently used to mean "the look" of something, as in the aesthetics of the living room or the aesthetics of the painting. Avoid this use.

Get rid of the abstract/figurative duality. It will not serve your work because it comes from an oversimplistic way of looking at art. Form/content is also a tiresome polarity. Instead, consider the friction between hand/distance, sublime/earthly, reference/presence, concept/object.

Reductivism *a priori* tends to end up in the wrong place. You can determine how much is enough when you understand what something needs. The sparseness of Zen paintings, for example, is the result of eliminating what can be eliminated, but no more. If the simplifying imperative has a clear thought and a moral sense behind it, the artwork will be sparse and authentic. Otherwise, even the most reductive work will be decorative and inauthentic.

In art, real knowledge is not what comes from hearsay, or what is gained by listening to the consensus, but what is unconcealed by deep engagement.

Art resists generalizations. Generalities undermine art and undermine the artist.

There are problems that are obvious to the artist and there are problems the artist does not grasp. Solutions for the second type of problem require a fundamental, sometimes paradigmatic, shift. Do you pose questions to yourself that could threaten your assumptions? Are clarity and knowledge the same? Can art clarify life?

Certain questions will arise in an honest mind that might not rise in a dishonest one. Certain answers will rise in a mind relatively free of calculations that might not rise in a mind used to weighing and planning. Nothing is neutral. Everything has a charge. A weight.

Fight against the trendy and against the reactionary. Both are too easy. The creative gesture is not the same as the whimsical gesture or the surprising flourish. Creativity is energy in search of a conduit.

Knowing how others acted in the face of a challenge is not the same as knowing how to act. A great deal of the knowledge we have is obtained through hearsay. We should try to add to this our own discoveries.

Sometimes thinking can get in the way of doing.

When you are looking at art, be where you are. Do not borrow a stance. Do not pretend.

Art reveals conflicts and possibilities that are obscured by language. Many false dualities arise from our attempts to use language to describe that which resists language.

Remaining authentic is not easy. Reconstruct the basis of judgment in each artwork.

Seriousness can at times be, both, insincere and a form of decoration. It can also be a place to hide.

The artist as prophet is different than the artist as mystic. The mystic goes to the mountaintop to gain insight, but does not come back. The prophet comes back. We do not need any more mystics, but we are in need of prophets.

Many judgments consist of one crude thought layered on top of another crude thought until a wall is built around the possibility of discovering something meaningful. Make an effort to get back to your foundation and build soundly upon it without fear the edifice of your judgments might not be impressive. And always let air in.

It is not hard to find reasons to laugh at the seriousness with which some artists approach their work. Cynicism comes easy to us. But that most art is decidedly insignificant in a world of calamities and beauty, does not mean all art is insignificant. These calamities and this beauty establish a benchmark and it is towards it you should aim your work. The proper reaction to the insignificance of most art in relation to the great tragedies and wonders of the world is not cynicism, but love and devotion.

Risk and Failure

Learn to live with risk and failure. Through them you discover whether or not you have the reserves you will need to move forward. Empowerment comes from insistence. As an artist, you need to risk much and fail often. You become more empowered every time you set out in the direction of greater risk. You disempower yourself when you play it safe.

An artist's practice should account for the uncertainty and instability that is always part of an honest inquiry. Expect change. Embrace accidents and mistakes.

The way to know you have gone too far is to go too far. At the boundary between the known and the unknown, either you leap or you retreat.

You do not know what you are capable of until you find the courage that lays dormant. Risk is the way. All you have suffered, lost, experienced, is brought forth by courage.

Real risk—as opposed to imagined or announced risk—is in proportion to what is at stake.

Your practice should rely on risk. If you do not know where to go, go in the direction of greater risk. Your willingness to take risks for what you know to be right is a measure of your courage and of your integrity.

In great works of art you will find success and failure next to each other. If you want the good far from the bad, you will have safety, but not art.

To be truly invested in your work means being willing to risk it for something better. If we cannot do that, then we are invested in ourselves, which is different than being invested in the work. The loss of an earlier stage of the work allows for the next one. Losses open possibilities.

Look at artists who are failing in the same way you are failing. Failure is sometimes easier to understand in someone else.

Adversity and failure allow you to find humility, strength, clarity, and new beginnings.

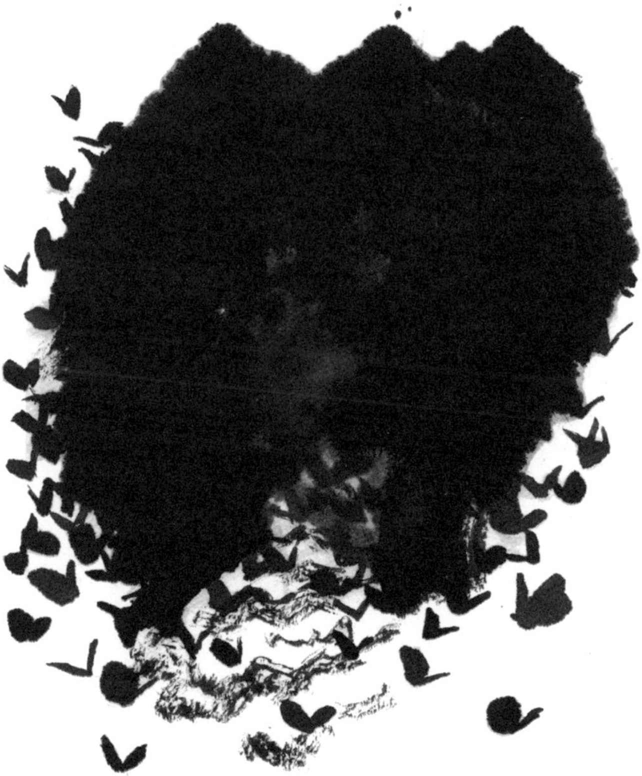

The making of any significant work involves subtlety, subversion against one's habits, and willingness to be wrong; sometimes catastrophically wrong.

A history of good decisions suggests, but does not guarantee, you will make good decisions in the future. Nothing guarantees that. Vigilance helps.

The vulnerability of a work can be its greatest strength. The vulnerability, even clumsiness, we sometimes see in great artworks comes from deep awareness of the way things work.

For every person who uses hardship as an excuse for not doing their artwork, there is always someone else who has done great work under similar circumstances.

One common way to waste time is to become insecure and self-defeating. It is often an excuse not to face the uncertainty of doing your work.

Play, self-discovery, religious commitment, therapy: these are often offered as excuses for not doing more difficult work.

The charming comes easily to those with taste and people with the right sensibilities can bring about the beautiful with a modest effort, but the sublime is another story. The sublime demands you walk away from the charming and from the beautiful through the rough passage of risk and dread.

What is threatening is not easily embraced, though you should embrace it. Success might seem to be in the hands of someone else, but it is in your hands.

Failure can bring about loneliness and sometimes it brings about the unbearable loneliness that comes with feeling worthless. When you find yourself there, do not run to the comfort of the known or negate yourself by trying to become someone else. Instead, consider the expectations you did not meet, try to understand their value for you, and set your course again.

Creating Your Work

The studio is the place where you work. The studio could be a big building, a small garage, a mountain, a computer, and in some rare cases, a mind.

The studio should amplify your sense of direction. Be careful not to make it only a collection of all your affectations and likings. Build it so the studio can teach you how to live and how to make choices. The way you are considering art should be the main studio question, not what you are going to do that day.

Place points of reference in your studio by which to measure your work. Part of your work is finding these references. Choose to keep around the things you can vouch for and stand behind. Confusion comes in when we strive to keep things or ideas we cannot really support.

Defend the clarity you need. Do not let people or things weaken your resolve. As an artist, create the space you need and recognize that those who love you may not understand.

In the studio you should not squander love or courage.

The studio is in the world. All your problems are artistic problems. The world illuminates your work and your work illuminates the world.

Your work should reflect who you are, where you are, and what you need. The right studio facilitates and amplifies the right vision. The wrong studio thwarts the spirit.

Sometimes it is wrong to push things and people away without knowing why, but sometimes you are right in doing so, even if you do not know the reason. Learning which moment is which is not easy. Art helps in understanding these choices.

Some questions or ideas lend themselves to investigation more easily than others. Sometimes investigating those questions or ideas that resist investigation can be very productive.

When you get stuck, when you cannot find the way in the studio, go to the studio anyway. Read there. Mop the floor. Rearrange things. Something will eventually happen.

Assemble your own tool kit based on destruction and rebuilding. In the tool kit there should be ideas to come back to as well as what to do when you are stuck and how to be comfortable in uncertainty. You accumulate these tools by working, by noticing how you overcome obstacles, and by watching other people work.

If you do not take yourself seriously, few people will. Respect your time, if you expect others to respect it.

You might be able to talk like an art historian or a critic, but when returning to the studio, collapse the distance critics and art historians tend to keep between themselves and the work.

Making means using your hands and it also means testing ideas with and against materials. To make something, you have to develop a relationship with the means involved and you have to come to terms with your role in regards to those means. It is not enough to say, "I will use paint or wood." Making is always about how something will be used.

It is worthwhile to think about the circumstances that allow art to happen or that prevent it from happening so you can create the right conditions. The questions, "Can it be done?" or "Does it challenge me?" are good places to start your work.

Take whatever approach you want to art making, but be sure it is the right one for you. You will know when your approach is the right one because it will challenge itself as well as you.

Creating a work of art ought to be a conversation between you and the work in which you are the quieter of the two. At some point when creating your work, there is a moment when you seem to disappear. This is the way.

If your work is not surprising you then there is more to do. The work should be many steps ahead of you.

Artists often ask, "When is an artwork finished?" It is finished when it has a life separate from your own.

Nothing guarantees you will create a great work of art. Art and doubt belong to the same camp. Art and guarantees belong to different camps.

Genius is not beforehand but becomes in the making.

A work of art can only be understood in its particulars and you as an artist need to distinguish those particulars. If you work in generalities, all you will have to offer is a sense of being sensitive, or worse, a sense of being tasteful.

There is usually more lying to oneself inside the studio than outside of it.

Sometimes it is useful not to be too attached to the work you are doing at the moment. It will change and hopefully it will deepen. Too much attachment will limit discovery. Ask yourself, "What will my work look like in twenty years?" If it will look like it does now, you ought to be disappointed.

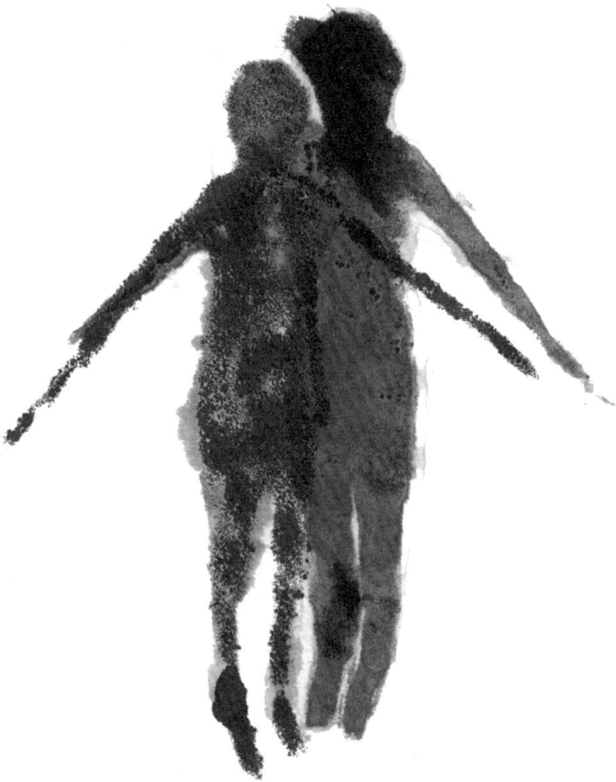

A painting is often more interesting at the beginning than at the end.

Painting starts with the preparation of the canvas—the weight of the canvas, the stretcher bars, the shape—and also with the paint, with the wall in your studio, etc. A painting, like all art, starts with your stance. In other words, a painting starts long before you begin to paint.

Allow for accidents to assist your intelligence. A responsive, critical stance to accidents increases your vision. Be open to every gesture. Perhaps it does not matter where you are going if where you are is better. Carelessness, however, does not consistently evolve into magic.

If art is a distraction for you, the work you make will also be a distraction.

Think broadly about color and fight your tendency to prefer certain colors. Look at colors in nature.

The most exciting images vacillate between meaning and meaninglessness. An artwork with meaning is not the same as a narrative artwork.

People tend to use the term "technically good" to signal that even when a work is missing something, it is, at least, well executed. But what does the term "technically good" possibly mean in art? It might mean something in an engagement where you can isolate the craft, but you cannot do that in art.

What do you mean by "the background?" In a painting everything is on the same plane. "The background" is around, not behind. We might be convinced the sky is really behind that great portrait of the young man in black by Giovanni Bellini, but the sky is next to his black hat. Nothing in a painting is behind anything else. Everything is next.

Sometimes it is useful to let the work go where it wants to go. This does not mean you are being mindless.

There are few things as impassive to your emotional contortions as art. Your politics and your kindness do not convince it, nor is it impressed by your status. It does not come forth just because you are living the right life.

Your materials and strategies should be the result of the questions you are asking. Why would you want to imitate anyone's questions? How would that serve you? Find your own. The materials will follow from there. Art is both materials and ideas. You should not lose sight of this duality.

Some people speak of distortions in artworks, such as what one might find in a late painting by Edvard Munch, but calling them distortions misses the point. Try to make a painting work as well as Munch's by distorting the figure and you will find out why calling them distortions misses the point.

Breakthroughs in your work often come from small subtleties. Can you transform your work by noticing some minor events or inconsistencies?

Ten misunderstood things added to each other does not equal one clear thing. It does not matter how many things are working in an artwork if the artwork is not good.

Many artists make artworks that are assemblies of parts. This part is good. This part is smart. This part I am attached to. And so on. The parts work at the expense of the whole. In a great work of art, on the other hand, there is always a gap between the whole and its parts. You should look at an artwork as a whole. Hold it in your mind as you work. Do not break it into parts.

It is useful to begin a work at a disadvantage. For an artist, what you do not know is a good point of departure.

Sometimes writing helps, not in explaining the work, but in coming to it with new awareness.

Work through assumptions—questions are not answered *a priori*. They are answered in doing the work.

In art, instead of responding to your limits and to your smallness, respond to whatever greatness is within you.

You do not have to try to self-express. Your responsibility is to clear out what is in the way. You also do not need to maintain a line of connection between all that you do. The line is always there.

One of the most difficult challenges for an artist is to know when the work is finished. There are no recipes, except perhaps: take it too far and you might recognize you should have stopped earlier.

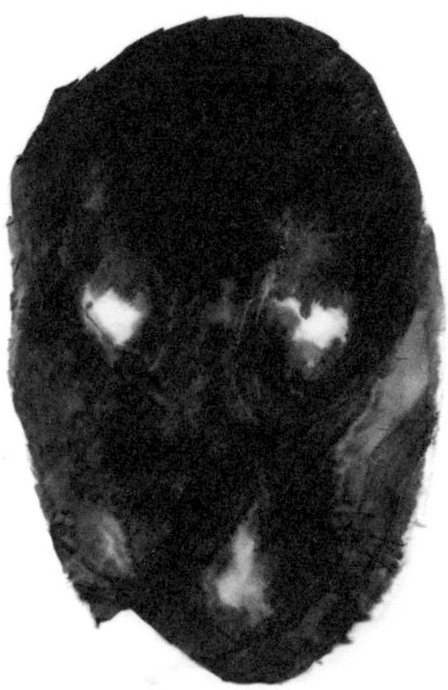

Dangers and Fears

The life of an artist is full of opportunity and discovery, but the many unknowns and the lack of models or conventions will mean you will have to face danger and deal with your own fear as well as with the fears of others. Often the greatest fear artists face is the fear of our own inadequacy, which makes us feel we are only pretending to be artists. This fear might make you quit or it might make you intensify the pretension, and neither of these responses is good. The best response is to recognize that, like your materials, fears are part of an artist's life and you must learn to work with them.

How can you corrupt or destroy possibilities? By hiding behind what is safe and known.

Be careful about keeping a foot in the real world. This foot weighs you down. When people tell you to be realistic, what they usually mean is you should hedge your bets, but art is rarely brought forth by people who consider themselves to be realistic. Be obstinate, but strive to be on both extremes of an argument at once.

In art, "almost there" does not count.

Do not hide your artistic frailties and weaknesses behind false *gravitas*. You are only be fooling yourself and those who are not serious. Shed the desire to be something you are not.

It is especially useful for the artist to free himself or herself from the need to appear intelligent. Trying to appear intelligent can be a form of apology. Art needs no apology.

Of course, there are many ways of working that are popular, and they are tempting because of the attention they receive. It comes down to what kind of artist you want to be and what you want to do with your time.

It is confusion and misunderstandings, especially of what we are, that hold us back from discovering what is in front of us.

What is confusing for some is exciting for others. A ship travels with relative safety through rocky seas when it is guided by a lighthouse at the shore. If there is no guide, a single, hidden rock can become a danger.

Some artists are eager to wedge themselves into the confusion of the art world. Take your time. Confusion will come regardless, but perhaps you will be prepared if you do not rush to find it.

We interpret our actions in ways that fit with our view of the world. Pay attention to what you do not want to know.

Many artists prefer to imitate than to live with the solitude and uncertainty of their own choices. Find the courage to remain on your course.

The facile might look austere and it might look wrought with work. An artist must struggle against easy answers.

The capacity to make fine distinctions is rare. It is also a source of confusion because often those who claim to have this capacity do not.

Do not dismiss someone just because they are doing the type of work you do not like.

You can probably find passages and ideas you admire in artworks you dislike, but these will not be enough. The spirit of an artwork is what runs underneath and also what binds all the surface activity, and it is that spirit that convinces you about an artist's work.

How can you stay vital? Study the world. Study yourself. But do not become an authority on either. Something secret, mysterious, must always remain.

There is a tendency to ask artists to consider their audience. You can find ways of creating bridges for the audience through conversations, books, and any other way that removes those barriers that can be removed, but be careful in crafting the work with an audience in mind. The audience is an abstraction and it changes. Also, the more you think of this imaginary group, the less present you tend to be in your own work.

Be mindful of how you use the word "express." Expressing suggests there is *a priori* location for something, but all great art has no precedent. It is always primary. It becomes.

Do not use any words that summarize conditions that ought to be treated in more detail—spiritual, existentialist, for example. Using these summarizing words will make you feel as if you know what is happening when, in fact, you do not. And not knowing but thinking you do is more dangerous than not knowing.

One problem with being under the spell of a certain way of thinking is that it narrows the field of possibilities.

Compromises allow you to move in the world, but they are not helpful in art. Be extreme. Be unreasonable.

We learn from other artists and we often imitate them, but do not imitate them for too long.

Do not suffocate your love with layers of justifications. Do not apologize for what you know is right.

Purposes change. Be aware. Private interest can be a trap. The purpose of a work is ultimately untouchable, but the use can be manipulated, changed, or misused.

Be suspicious any time elegance comes easily.

Be attentive to it, but do not become enamored with your idea. Loving whatever comes out of your hand is dangerous. Artists tend to either be enamored with their own hand or deeply insecure—often at the same time.

There will be a number of deaths in your evolution as an artist. Do not mourn them for very long.

The myth of the artist as an idiot savant is unfortunate.

Be protective of your work, but be detached from it. Resist the temptation to praise your work or its preciousness. Resist adjectives. Forget compliments. Avoid grandiose words when speaking about your work. Also avoid being vague. And especially, avoid being vague while using grandiose words.

Few people wake up in the morning and say, "Today I am going to sell out." Selling out, giving up on your dream, your integrity, usually happens slowly, imperceptibly, over time. A little compromise here. Another one there. One day you are too busy. The next you are being reasonable. Then you are trying to fit it in. You tell yourself you have responsibilities, that you are accountable to many people. Many of the steps you take will make sense and some will seem righteous and necessary. But eventually there you are: a shadow of what you used to be. Be vigilant. Be courageous. Recognize the choices you are making and why you are making them.

Towards a Practice

An artistic practice is anything we do regularly—rituals, habits, tasks—that supports our work as artists. Unlike theories or beliefs, a practice is revealed less by what is said than by what is done and perhaps even more by how it is done.

Creativity often comes from survivals skills, from having to solve problems in inventive ways because you did not have more obvious means at your disposal. Many people tend to associate creativity with freedom and moving laterally across a field of possibilities; in fact, creativity is frequently a response to limits and it usually demands a vertical, deeper incursion into the material.

Let doubt be a source of growth rather than a debilitating force. If you want to maintain your integrity, question yourself often. Doubt your best deeds. Examine your smallness. Doubt is at the heart of any serious artistic practice as well as the day-to-day activities of an artist. Some artists think the doubts will eventually subside, but they will not. As you mature, new questions appear that challenge whatever development you have attained.

Constantly push against yourself and against what you have been. Nothing good comes without a rupture, without a tear in your view of the world. Cultivate those ruptures. A linear path will not take you where you need to go—some fracture has to happen.

Identify the people in the world who can be your friends and who respect your effort. Find a mentor alive or dead. You can find guidance in books. Try to build a standard by extrapolating the values you have learned from those you admire. If you are lucky enough to find a mentor who is alive, then put yourself at his or her service. It is not necessary to bring up art and do not ask your mentor to look at your work. It is not important what you do together because what you need to learn is how your mentor is in the world. Art will eventually follow.

The company you keep matters. Do not underestimate the dangers of spending time with people of less integrity than you, and do not overestimate your virtue. If possible, be around artists who are better than you and who hold themselves to a higher standard. Be around them even if you do not talk about art. Sometimes it is better not to.

In response to an invitation to write an article, Robert Henri remarked "a cobbler should stick to his last," and he goes on to explain how a painter should put all his energies in what he or she does best, which in his case was painting. This outlook is right for some artists, but not for all artists. In the case of Leonardo, all the other activities he did enriched his understanding of the world and led to greater paintings. Part of your work is figuring out what kind of artist you are and what you need to fuel and challenge your work.

Do not worry about stripping down the work. Strip yourself down—worry about that.

Be inventive. See what something can become. Find what something wants to be.

Holding a personal position with the weight of years of experience behind it might or might not be good. Accumulation of years, in itself, is not a credential. For some, life is a process of learning and of opening. For others, it is a process of covering the moment with cobwebs of familiarity.

You might want your work to reflect your political views and there is nothing wrong with that, but art is rarely an effective way to do politics. The gallery and museum audience will probably praise you, yet you will not change much.

Having a sense of what you do not want to paint is helpful. So, work on discovering what you want to leave out.

Pulling away from the work looks easy, but it is not. In fact, it is one of the biggest challenges in anyone's practice.

Reading a secondary text in, say, philosophy, is a good way to learn about the thoughts of a great mind, but to learn how a great mind thinks you must read primary works. There you will find how a mind moved through a problem. While reading, ask yourself, "How did this mind pass through the world?" It is similar with a work of art. Nothing replaces immediate experience. Viewing artworks in books has little to do with the experience of being with them.

You can, and you must, define your own journey. Learn from others, but be aware of the solitude of your actions. This is your life. Do not give it away.

To pursue a goal requires perseverance and strategy. Getting a clear understanding of the use of your work is important for removing inner confusion. Clarify to yourself what is at stake for you and what is at stake for your work. Clarity of mind is more important than whatever you are attached to.

Be willing to take out aspects of your work when they are no longer necessary. You may have needed a ladder to climb to a certain place, but when you are there, let it go.

Do not hold on too long to things you do not need. Feel the anxious calling of your future work. Move on. But also always make your art from where you stand without pretending to be more advanced than you are. For better or for worse, you are where you are.

Launch yourself recklessly towards your dreams. Wake up and be desperate. Desperation demands action. As an artist, you must always be desperate. Try anything. Be careful with your calculations. Calculations become a habit. A calculated life is seldom radiant.

When you feel you are all over the place try to find a different vantage point. Sometimes there is another plane of thought where disparate ideas reconcile or, at least, coexist.

You have to work on your strengths as well as on your weaknesses. Strengths can lead to habits and over-familiarity. Lean on your weaknesses from time to time. Shake your strengths, strengthen your weaknesses. Sometimes the skills we need are those we do not want to learn.

Your practice should be centered on inquiry and there will be times when your inquiry is of little interest to others. Most of the time, this points to your delusion, but sometimes, this means you are on the right track.

Enrich your reservoir of ideas and possibilities by knowing more. Know the artists and thinkers you admire and know why you admire them. If your admiration rises from your weaknesses, from your smallness, then find new people and new ideas to admire. Those who you admire should call you to be better. They should not justify where you are.

Look at many artworks and learn how they were made; not just materially, but also the choices that were made—what was left in and what was taken out. The algebra of those choices is what you need to understand.

Let the light of poetry and literature reflect on your art practice. Read not only for content, but also to learn structure, strength of character, and worldview.

The poetic is not flowery. Good poetry always has dirt grinding between its gears.

Question your purpose. Let it change if you need to. Do not feel obligated to what you believed yesterday, but also, do not be careless with your past efforts. There is an ideal yet precarious equilibrium between seeing each day as new and respecting where you have been. It is natural to feel obliged to your past work and to the statements you have made, but your biggest debt is to the future.

To maintain your integrity as an artist you should remove the word "style" from your vocabulary. When you think of using it, ask yourself what you mean and say that. Do not hide your assumptions under a word. Do not feel obligated to a word.

What is the division between you and your work? Between your life and your practice? Think about these divisions.

Artists must resist all dogmas and groups. Often the most dangerous of these dogmas is the one you have created yourself. Standards and dogmas are not the same thing. Your practice should help you distinguish between the two.

You should have no allegiances to anything, except to what you estimate to be great, even if that greatness is but a dim beacon far away. Nothing is so precious or so right that it cannot be reconsidered.

If you keep fiddling with an artwork to protect the part you like, scrape it out. Start over. Do not tweak. Sometimes throwing work away is necessary. By sacrificing a work you like in search of something better, you learn what it means to be an artist.

The temptation to settle threatens your efforts to make fine distinctions. Do not give up. When you feel yourself getting tired seek help in friends or books.

You must be a student of your work, but never an expert. Leave room for the unknown, for the surprise.

There is a secret in all things. If you keep this in mind you will not go far off course.

Beyond the Studio

In one way or another, your work and yourself will always have to contend with the world. Sometimes the decisions you make in the studio become untenable when your work goes beyond the studio. Other times your work is embraced and it appears all your decisions were the right ones. Occasionally, it is your attitude as an artist that seems indefensible and the reasons why are not always clear. In any case, the dynamics of your work in the world will play a role in your life one way or another, so it is best to be aware of and responsive to that role.

You want to find a place in the world for you and for your work, so take this aim seriously and do not accept what others are doing as your model if it does not feel right for you.

There is a time to read, a time to look, and a time to experience. There is also a time to work and a time to rest. Sometimes these periods overlap. Sometimes they do not. Understand where you are.

There are times in an artist's life when he or she should not publicly show work. These are times of cooking and simmering. Only you know when you are ready to go public, but do not let fear or impatience make the decision for you.

If you want to show your work, ask yourself why. The answer might reveal where you are.

Exhibitions are not passive unveilings. You should think of them as part of the development of the work.

You need to know your work well enough to understand how and where to show it. A gallery might seem like a showroom, but it is not one. A gallery is a context and a partner. Be aware of what you are doing if you place your work in galleries you do not respect or that you are pretending to respect.

When you are ready to show your work, but you do not have a track record, you could say, "I have not done many exhibitions, but here is my work." Many dealers, curators, and collectors will dismiss you, but if your work is good, someone will notice.

Try to create bridges to the audience, but avoid the wink of shared jokes or insights.

Many artists are worried about appearing to be self-promoting. "I am not a salesman," they say proudly, and so they relinquish control of their work and its framework to a gatekeeper. Perhaps they think they are being true to their work when, in fact, it is often the opposite. Instead of promoting, create points of entry into your work so you do not have to trust a gatekeeper to explain it.

It is better to devise ways to create a context for someone else and offer points of entry than to explain or translate your work.

Your work is interesting only to you: this should be your assumption when you place your work in the world. You are likely to be right. If you put your work in the world and no one looks at it, that in itself is feedback. Schools and workshops create artificial interest. The first thing your work has to conquer is not rejection but indifference.

The viewer completes the endeavor. There is no work of art without the viewer.

Your audience will reveal itself, though not always right away.

The most common problem in artists' statements is the disparity between purpose and action. Multiple, even contradictory desires can be brought together, but that does not mean they function well together or that anything worthwhile will be brought about. You might want to drag several ideas and invent a narrative about how they work, but just because you wish something, does not mean that it is.

The language we use to talk about art is often inadequate. It is a good idea to work on the way we talk. If for nothing else, to recognize what we do not understand. Many problems in art are the by-product of confusions introduced by language. Beginning a sentence with, "I like this..." is suspicious and usually irrelevant.

Do not compromise your work to fit in, but do not confuse lack of popularity with greatness.

During studio visits, it is better to be quiet than to speak too much. Err on the side of saying less. Read the signs. End it if it is not right for you.

Think carefully about how you present yourself to the world. Everything is the work. Nothing is outside of it.

The words "transcendence" and "spiritual" are losing their meaning because they are so often misused. It is best to avoid them in describing your work. They are summary words. Instead, say what you mean without the summary. Also, avoid saying things like "I am challenging the viewer to…" The people you should be accounting for are those whom you cannot challenge with self-impressed insights.

Learn to navigate your success as well as your rejections. Sometimes a success, even a little success, is more dangerous than a rejection.

When things seem to be going very well, remember it is difficult to tell the difference between a groove and a rut.

You might get tired of battling with your work while trying to find recognition for it. This fatigue eats at your dreams and can make you do things you never thought you would do. You will see others in bright lights while you endeavor in the dark. You will mark your birthdays with anxiety, "When is this going to happen for me?" You might be holding another job to pay for what sometimes feels like an addiction or a waste of time. We cannot pretend this is an easy situation to deal with, but perseverance offers its own rewards. One of them is self-respect.

Every bad work you put into the world is a missed opportunity.

While there are many posers in the mainstream artworld, many of the best artists, critics, curators and gallerists are also there. If you shun the mainstream in search of something more authentic, chances are you are going down a rabbit hole from which you will never come back, and your work will suffer for it.

Most of our opinions are trapped in our time. Often we agree with each other not because we are right, but because our basis for judgment is similar.

Reflect on the spirit of the age and consider whether what you are doing fits in or does not. There are ways to handle yourself either way, but you ought to know where you stand.

It is impossible for any field of knowledge to continue to exist on its own and the arts are, in many ways, irrelevant to the contemporary development of knowledge and ideas. When we see groupings like *Arts & Leisure* we begin to understand where we are. Why not, *Arts & Knowledge* or *Arts & Labor*? The separation of art from other endeavors is part of the reason why we, artists, find ourselves without a useful role in society, other than, as jesters and commodity makers.

If dissent is expected, even enshrined, as it is in the canon of contemporary art, how do you dissent, and what would you be dissenting against?

The success of science in the last 150 years has created an inferiority complex in all other disciplines, which prompts them to pretend to be scientific. And so, those aspects of art that resist the scientific treatment, such as immediacy and authenticity, are pushed aside.

When trying to communicate with others, science and art share the challenge of using a language under stress. For the most part, words do not serve us well when speaking about what really matters in art or science, so we are forced to speak in generalities.

We tend to admire those who can do things without much effort. The detached genius has great appeal, and yet it seems we are invested in our work to the extent we invest ourselves.

When you step into a museum, most paintings will remain firmly anchored to their historical condition, but not the great works of art. These will leap at you and meet you where you are. They are ahistorical, even those with a historical reference, like Goya's *The Shooting of May 3rd*.

Handling success can be as treacherous as handling failure. Many people who seem indomitable and willing to risk everything become soft and safe once they reach their first set of goals. It is easy to complain about the establishment and maintain an irreverent attitude when success and wealth have not brought you to a comfortable place. Many say, "I won't be corrupted," but experience shows us something different.

Navigating a career is not easy. Expect to be thrown about by rejections, indignities, and by your own ambitions. You will be challenged by the sacrifices you and those around you have to make, and you are likely to be battered by the uncertainty of whether these sacrifices are worth the potential rewards. The success of others will make you anxious and the effervescence of art fairs, rankings, superstars, and money will be tempting. The wind of confusion will always be blowing against you and monsters of one sort or another, like poverty or disillusionment, wait to ambush you around the bend. You will have to contend with your own doubts and limitations as well as the loneliness that comes with setting yourself upon the artist's course in the first place. To keep at it with dignity and without bitterness, find beacons that guide you and meanings that sustain you.

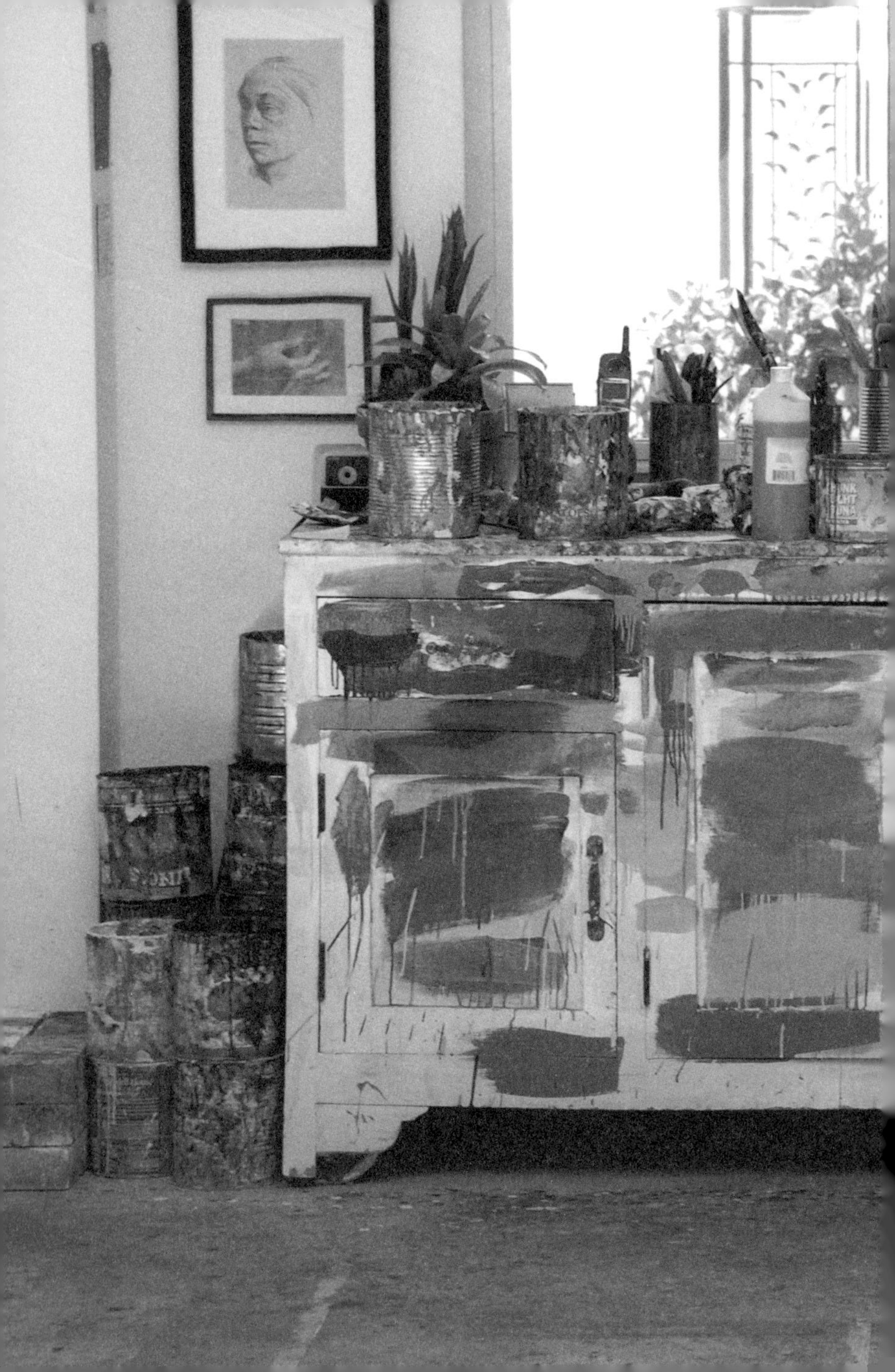

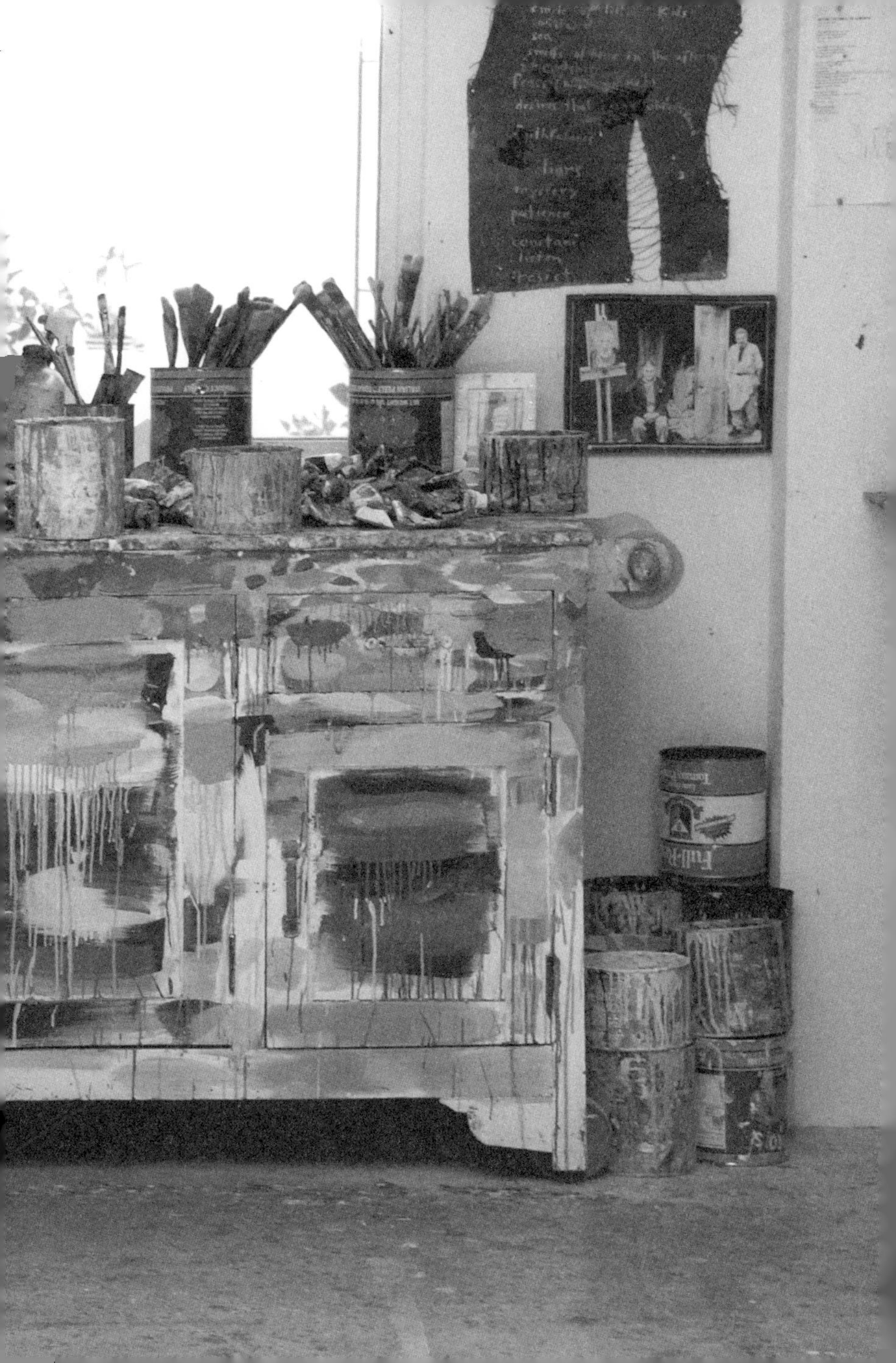

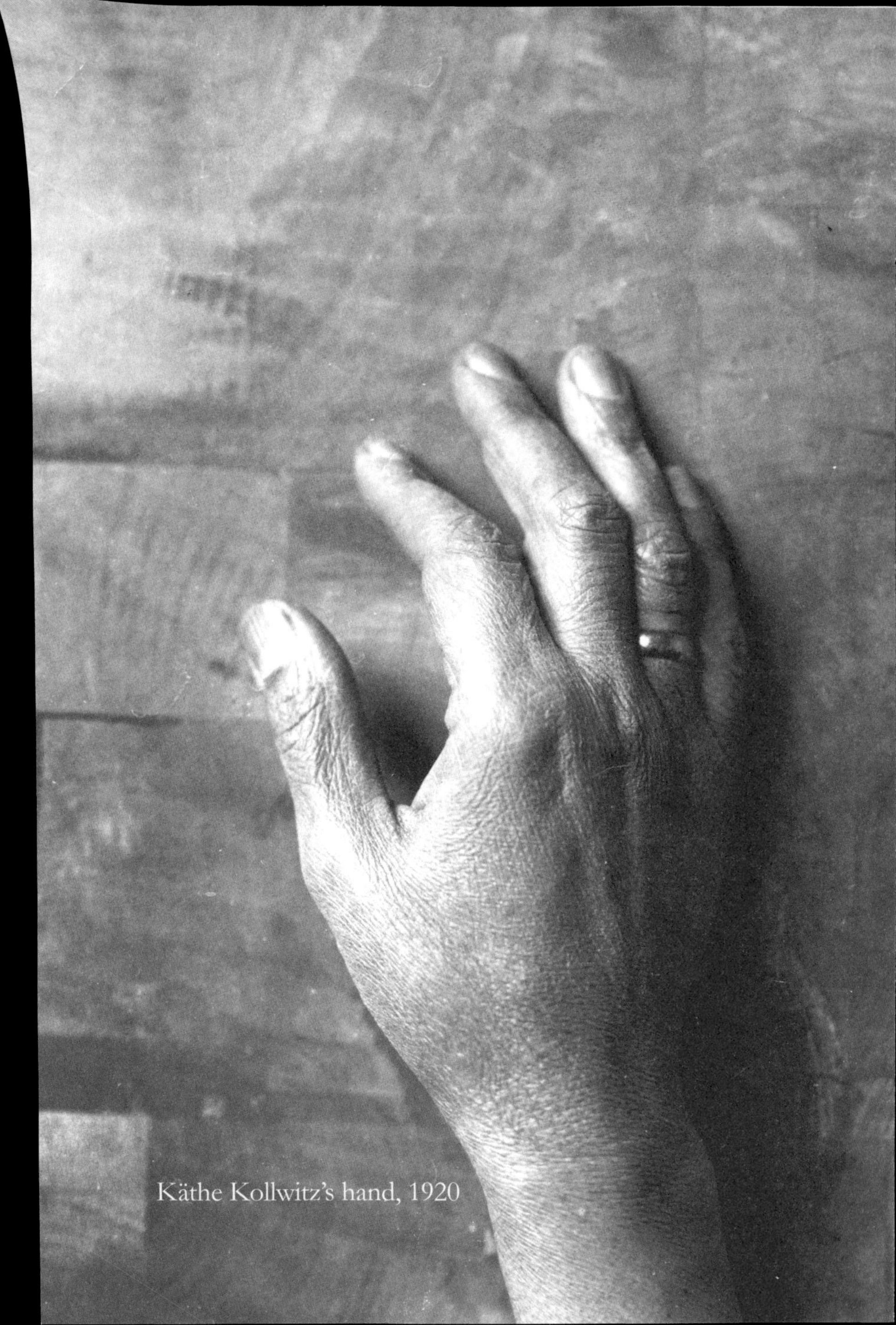

Käthe Kollwitz's hand, 1920

Afterword

An artist is a perishable idea. That someone is an artist today does not mean this will be true tomorrow. He or she might still work, dress, and speak like an artist, but when the flame that warmed actions and illuminated thoughts is no longer burning, the artist loses his or her way and the work becomes cold. Edvard Munch wrote in 1933, "I was aware of the fact that my torch flamed up, then was almost extinguished, and I gazed around in darkness and fear. I had lost my way. Who was I? Had I lost my way for good? But I managed to rekindle my torch, and drag myself from the undergrowth. I fell and I ran. I sought my way on broken limbs. Where was the path?"[2] In Munch's case, the flame came back after it was almost extinguished, but this rekindling is rare. More often, the flame is extinguished permanently without announcements or deference for social frameworks, spiritual conviction, or personal devotion.

That it can flicker and disappear suggests the energy of the flame is not solely a function of talent, which is a more stable attribute. Talent is important and it would be hard to find a great artist who was not talented, but the initial spark that makes an artist an artist ignites in the friction between talent and character. Character is reflected in the artist's will to move through the world with keen eyes, skeptical of his or her gains, and eager to accept responsibility as an individual. Character is also reflected in the artist's capacity to manage the solitude in which many of the important choices must be made and in his or her fortitude in the face of long-delayed rewards, insecurity, and limitations.

Although there are thousands of writings about character, and much has been said about integrity, we frequently see artists trade their solitude for acceptance or ease. But these choices are not inevitable. However difficult it might be, we could aim to live, as Friedrich Nietzsche wrote, "above ourselves in order that we may be able to live with ourselves."[3]

The solitude I am referring to is not the isolation of idealisms and retreats, which do not only escape the absurdity of markets and trends, but also the reality of the world as it is. The artist who does not want to become over-familiarized with, and ultimately calcified in, his or her own opinions and views, cannot remain apart but must continue to work in dialog with society.

But we must be vigilant. Being in the world requires consciousness of our surroundings and that consciousness can sometimes lead to insecurity and conformism. Perhaps the artists and the art of our time are not worse than those of any other period, but the contemporary contrast between the enormous market-educational apparatus built around the arts and the lack of ambition of much of the work we see makes our time seem especially dangerous to the perishable idea that is an artist.

One of the biggest threats confronting the artist today is the illusion that the exceptional and the uncommon are revered. Institutions, galleries, critics, and collectors now seem driven to uncover and praise novelty; originality and dissent (of the kind that is nonthreatening to structures of power) may have become trendy, but nothing has changed for artists who seek truth in and through their work. The exceptional and the uncommon may be the ends for the artist whose flame has been extinguished, but for the artist whose flame shines brightly, the exceptional and the uncommon remain the means.

The advice that matters most then is to remain mindful of the flame, an advice that is hard to implement without examples. I hope this book can provide a few—examples I myself need and use daily.

Enrique Martínez Celaya
Los Angeles, California, 2015

Notes

[1] Camus, Albert. *Resistance, Rebellion, and Death.* New York: Knopf, 1961. 106.

[2] Martínez Celaya's sketchbook, 2003. Original source unknown.

[3] Thiele, Leslie Paul. *Friedrich Nietzsche and the Politics of the Soul: A Study of Heroic Individualism.* Princeton, N.J.: Princeton University Press, 1990. 194.

Illustrations

13, workshop participants with EMC, Anderson Ranch Arts Center, 2012; 29, 36, 38, 55, 66, 71, ink on mulberry paper, 2015; 106-107, painting table at the artist's studio, 2008; 108, Käthe Kollwitz photograph, 1920.

First published in hardcover in the United States of America by Whale & Star Press, Culver City, California. www.whaleandstarpress.com

Design: Whale & Star Press
Lead Publication: Tessa Blumenberg and Mary Strebinger
Copy: María Teresa Bonilla, Tessa Blumenberg, and Elizabeth Williams
Cover: Enrique Martínez Celaya, photograph from *Guide*, 2002
Distributed exclusively by University of Nebraska Press
1111 Lincoln Mall, Lincoln, Nebraska 68588-0630
www.nebraskapress.unl.edu
Tel: 800/755 1105

ISBN: 978-0-9799752-9-5